MW00398110

This book belongs to:

____

Made in the USA
Coppell, TX
04 January 2021

47552559R10066